MARÍA FÉLIX

© 2006 Assouline Publishing
601 West 26th Street, 18th floor
New York, NY 10001, USA
Tel.: 212 989-6810   Fax: 212 647-0005
www.assouline.com

Translation from the French by Jeanine Herman

Photoengraving by Gravor (Switzerland)
Printed by Grafiche Milani (Italy)

ISBN: 2 84323 888 9

MARÍA FÉLIX

PIERRE PHILIPPE

ASSOULINE

That face. That face, first of all. Almost perfectly rectangular with a rounded forehead at its summit, surrounded by the hair of a Gorgon; hair tamed in long, dark waves or—when the role demanded it—in arabesques as glossy as weapons, leathery spirals, nocturnal ramparts. A face that comes from a distant land, in which one can see, behind the most outrageous makeup, the Indian complexion and the elasticity of the skin over a bone structure taken from some Mayan mask. A face that was made for a close-up, in a time when infatuated cameramen would spend hours sculpting women with light, to the sound of a small orchestra, women like Francesca Bertini, Greta Garbo, and Zarah

María Félix in *Les héros sont fatigués* by Yves Ciampi, 1955.
Raymond Boyer Collection. Photograph: Roger Corbel © Ministry of Culture.

Leander. A face that escaped from the ancient fascination of silent film, where only the enormous eyes had something to say, and the fascinating play of the brushstrokes of her eyebrows, two dark bird's wings concealed under the formidable forehead, and whose imperceptible or wrathful quivering alone compensated for the deficiencies of the dialogue, issued almost regretfully from a fruity but always contemptuous mouth.

The face of a dominatrix, a huntress, a carnivore. The jawbone does not lie. It does not open to smile, almost never to laugh candidly, free of ulterior motives. And it is certainly true that goddesses of this sort do not have the desire, or the leisure, to share man's distinguishing feature with partners whose hearts they are busy breaking, whose body and soul they are tearing to pieces. And because this Olympian beauty (with the beauty of Venus, certainly, but also that of the austere Juno) is made more human by a small flaw, childhood maliciously left the twinkling of a beauty mark on all this cold harmony, right in the center of her left cheek—an unexpected detail which Félix's makeup artists would play up to great effect when it was time to add spice to a mask that seemed destined for relentless perfection.

but this face is merely the impressive preamble to the eloquence of an entire body; through the felicitous blessing of the dates of her passage into the cinematic arts, María Félix avoided the inevitable temptations to repeatedly exhibit herself. She is from the era when the neckline of a dress slipping over a shoulder, caressed by the backlighting of a projector, is equal to a whole sequence of our contemporary orgies. Her chest was not subject to vulgar voyeurism. It would be solicited, however, in every possible way, expressly thrust out to the limits of indiscretion, imagined in the slight opening of her shawls, which were less knotted than viewers' throats, and spilling most generously out of the turn-of-the-century corsets tightened to the point of asphyxiation. There, again, her supple skin, like silken fabric, was marvelous, whether brutally denuded by the proletarian hands of Yves Montand and revealed —from behind—to the waist in the film *Les Héros sont fatigués* (1955), or, more subtly, in *French Cancan* (1954), when Jean Renoir decided to inscribe the lustful undulation of Lola de Castro's hips in Technicolor, the "beautiful Abbess" moving before a living curtain of soldiers, in imitation of the famous courtesans of 1900, Cléo de Mérode and Liane de Pougy.

these are the two poles to which French cinema would relegate this beauty exotic: a creature, likely a prostitute, haunting the seedy bars of a Latin America imagined by set decorators at the Boulogne-Billancourt, Paris studios; and rigged up, ornate, like a luxury hearse. Her undressing, as Jean Cocteau wrote, was planned and executed like a house moving. Moreover, a few months before *French Cancan* was filmed, an unimaginative screenwriter and mediocre director wrapped *La Belle Otero* (1954), one of those Franco-Italian follies, with biographical claims, that viewers on a Saturday night in 1955 enjoyed thoroughly; watching it today is only made bearable by the appearance of Félix in the splendid costumes of Marcel Escoffier. By what strange paths did this marvel of the Mexican screen, this icon—already—for everyday audiences as well as the most demanding intellectuals of her country, manage to tarnish her image in the often dubious productions that Europe offered her? How did she, beauty of beauties, not choose the charms of Hollywood, as her glorious predecessor Dolores del Río had? And then, what would María's undoubtedly different destiny have been: this is where the mysteries of her private life arise, and also, no doubt, the imbroglios of the politics of agents to the stars —entanglements as mysterious, indeed, poisonous, as those of some stars today. Whatever the case, this was the moment when Félix—sanctified for Europeans by the photogenic, cloud-filled skies captured by chief cameraman Gabriel Figueroa—took her legend and set off for Paris, as well as Madrid and Rome, with the hope, perhaps, of eclipsing the Italians who were cornering the market at the time, namely Gina Lollobrigida and Sophia Loren.

One could, of course, dream up a more poetic version of the facts, one that would make María Félix the new, natural, historic link between Mexican culture and the cultures in these parts of old Europe. She would appear in the prestigious splendor of the great twentieth-century adventurers who spent their life trying, without great success, to weave together the sizzling threads of a disheveled, Latin American romanticism with those infinitely more tepid aspects of our most daring aesthetic revolutions. Yes, these thoughts are less absurd than they seem: imagine María Félix as a galleon with billowing sails transporting the golden treasure of the Aztecs in her sides, coming to Europe as a sublime ambassador of the soul of her country. She would embody a glittering response from one continent to the other, a living reply to the mad love so dear to the French surrealist André Breton, and which he also felt for Mexico (after the playwright Antonin Artaud), and thought was embodied in the painterly, mythic couple formed by Diego Rivera and Frida Kahlo, themselves wrapped in the shadow of a perfect couple cast in the revolutionary ideal of Leon and Natalia Trotsky, exiled to Mexico by Stalin. Absurd? Not at all. That would be to forget that for a while María was the third side of a love triangle, the most surrealist love triangle imaginable by the pope of this new religion of excess, and part of the famous derangement of all the senses preached by the French poet Rimbaud. The two visual artists intertwined their names with the actress's in a garland that is remarkable to see today, along the walls of Frida's bedroom, where they no doubt drank in her youthful splendor in their respective ways.

t he absolute, timeless beauty linked to this brilliant duo —Rivera, the great muralist painter sustained by Marxism and Kahlo, the morbid self-portraitist beset by physical catastrophe—sparked the imagination, with its naturally provocative derivations into a barely admissible eroticism. Needless to say, this ménage à trois—surrealist or not—fueled speculation and daydreams for a long time, without troubling María very much. In any case, what taboos, what borderline experiences could make her recoil, this woman who was not afraid to say, whenever she got the chance, that her appearance was not to be trusted, that she had always considered herself a man in a woman's body, and that as a teenager, she had dreamt of enslaving her adored brother, Pablo?
With this mythology in place, we should go back to a much less lyrical reality. We should linger for a while on the vital struggle

that Félix was always candid about, well before her life as an actress. The war started early on, when she ran away from a family of twelve children, in which the girls were meant to blindly obey rules that would prepare them for lives of subservience and fertility. She was already a rebel, neglecting her dolls to fight with the boys and soon winning her independence from the natural path of all her peers: obscure and humiliating projects, beauty contests, and a marriage at sixteen to Enrique Álvarez who would introduce her to the horrors of male brutality but also give her the joy of a son.

On this short path that brought her from Sonora, the mining province where she was born in 1914 (to Josefina Güereña and Bernardo Félix) in Guadalajara, where her youthful beauty was already turning heads (those of the older men she would always fascinate, as well as those of the students who elected her queen of the university), to the capital, Mexico City, where she would languish as a typist, eager to change her status, María had already accumulated a number of important lessons regarding the code of what would now be the philosophy of her existence.

So without too much hand-wringing, she allowed herself to be approached on the street by a Fernando Palacios, who promised nothing less than to propel her to the firmament of Mexican cinema—then at the height of its power—in the company of the biggest male star of the time, Jorge Negrete. This had to be one of those dubious propositions with which the road is paved for a young, dark-haired woman aware of all eyes upon her. But what did María have to fear? She was beautiful, she was poor, and she had suffered horribly at the hands of her husband,

Álvarez, when he absconded with their young son, Enrique, her "Quique". This was 1941, the world over there, far away, was at war, and María decided to launch her own campaign against misery and anonymity. So she accepted the invitation, with its risks and its perils. The miracle was that Palacios's proposition was not a trap, or rather it was a splendid trap, in this world of illusions Félix was now entering, not as a frail, dazzled gosling, but as a woman of 25, a young mother, a part-time actress whose life had already given her the lessons in comedy—and tragedy—required to practice this new craft. Negrete, naturally, turned on the charm. To everyone's surprise—and to the actor-singer-star's, most of all—she resisted him and was arrogant, even hateful. He would forgive her ten years later, when, becoming more than his equal, she chose him on her own accord; their wedding was practically a holiday for the entire Mexican nation.

While waiting for the tables to turn, their film —María's first—entitled *El Peñón de las Animas* (1942), directed by Miguel Zacarías, was a huge success, one of those gems that the Mexican cinema would extract from its national enclave and propel onto the global stage, starting a golden age in which María Félix clearly already had an eminent place—her own.

This striking primacy might have been darkened by the prestige of the legendary Dolores del Río, who had opted for Hollywood's mirages and dollars more than fifteen years earlier. But the only international star of Mexican birth stayed in California (returning to her country the following year to gather her own laurels in the new cinema); she was ten years older than María, with an innate passiveness, a dolorousness, that the musical comedies she agreed to appear in never really allowed one to forget; in short, she seemed overtaken by the newcomer with her restrained ardor, her animal-like energy under surveillance, the flash of her eyes, the gleam of her teeth, and the promises of her anatomy.

By her third film, *Doña Barbara* (1943), by Fernando de Fuentes, María Félix was already inscribed in her own young legend. Its ingredients were the same as those of twenty Mexican films to come: a young peasant woman, raped by a band of thugs, reappears a reel later, improbably transformed into a wealthy heiress, an Amazon in a black hat and tie, galloping across her fields, in the aridity of which poor men are ridiculed, whipped, and abandoned to the most degrading fate. María's entire mythography was already present here, and her unwavering desire for revenge against those who had seduced and abused her, like her ex-husband, Enrique Álvarez, led to this sought-after, triumphant detachment.

b ut ten films and four years later, it was in the sumptuous *Enamorada* (1946) that María Félix—and Mexican cinema as a whole—would find the exact point of their appeal: specifically, the ever fragile, troubling, almost romantic relationship between an audience and the artists who try to win them over. The great Emilio "Indio" Fernandez was at the controls of this machine, setting in motion the picturesque, revolutionary folklore of the beginning of the century. And it was Pedro Armendáriz, that virile hunk of Latin sex appeal, who was chosen to oppose, and then unite with, a Félix brought to the incandescence of her lofty beauty. The two slaps she administers to the ruffian he plays entered instantly into the whole anthology of Mexican cinema.

No detail was neglected, as a whole spectrum of feminine attributes taken from popular imagery, from the painting of her friends Rivera and Kahlo, was deployed around María—with the serpentine suppleness of her body, her face sculpted with delicate shadows by the brilliant cameraman Gabriel Figueroa, sublimating the sparkling whites of her eyes lidded in the throes of passion. It was all heavy, glossy tresses embellished with satin bows, abundant lace, pearls, and clattering pendants. And in the end, this shedding of petticoats, cast off to the rhythm of a horse's trot, her long, loose hair blending with their manes, showed us that submission to the male order was accepted, though the actress still infused it with so much internal violence, like the landscapes she traveled across and from whose flat horizon a cactus or sisal plant would occasionally rise up.

here, Félix was an ardent *soldadera*, the female soldier, holding firmly to the saddle of her man's steed, a man reduced to the ideogram of his vast sombrero, arched silhouette, and cartridge pouches. An emblematic image of Mexican cinema, offered in eternal gratitude to the Soviets who came to the country not long ago to advocate their revolution and put their brilliance in the service of the Republic—director Sergei Mikhailovich Eisenstein and his French cameraman Edouard Tissé; an epic image tempered by a certain glamour taken from Hollywood, in which María Félix is resplendent, though one might wonder whether the actress was, in private, a *pasionaria*, or fervent revolutionary, of this sort. Wasn't she the female part of a restless duo at the time formed with Agustín Lara, the continent's most famous melodist, a charmer with a mummified face whose refrains made hearts beat more quickly, including—for seven years—María's. With Lara, she threw herself into singing and, in spite of limited means, had successes in all Spanish-speaking countries. He wrote "María Bonita" for her, which in a single day became the national anthem of seduction. And especially for her—because it was a wound that had to be closed—he arranged to retrieve Enrique, her now adolescent son, whom María found again like a lost treasure and who would now become, through all the twists and turns of her life, the only man in whom she would find true love and comfort when she subjected to the affronts that did not fail to punctuate her adventurous path.

meanwhile, she understood—she said so herself—that her work as an actress, and hence her status as a star, was not what she had initially envisioned when she started out. But the easy money, and so much of it, gave her the power to retrieve her beloved Quique and to prove to the world that she could raise him by herself and give him the best education. She knew now that she had to be credible, taking on more complex roles than those that required her animal grace alone. And she also felt, intuitively, that she had become an idol with the arduous task of giving some substance to the films that relied on her to exist. Because she was among those rare women who needed only a slim pretext to enrapture the public and set fire to its imagination. Like Garbo or Dietrich, she was a star whose surroundings could be shabby but whose resplendence was all the more absolute.

These were great years for Félix and for Mexico. Under the presidency of Miguel Alemán Valdés, the country seemed to emerge from its provincialism, and with the aid of the United States, Mexico's architectural, literary, pictorial, and cinematic history attained great heights. All signs indicated, however, that this state of grace could not last forever and that, as far as the art of the screen went, the days were numbered for the vaguely tainted enchantments of the films in which María reigned. Now the stories dominating the box office were romps involving streetwalkers, rumba dancers with an aggressive vulgarity, and "victims of sin" played by actresses such as Amalia Aguilar and Ninón Sevilla, which eclipsed the candid hymns to Zapata and the oppressed peasantry of the years of struggle.

there was also no doubt why María Félix, fine strategist that she was, decided to broaden her horizons, to abandon her state of absolute national diva and take the risk of setting sail on the seas of international cinema. She divorced Agustín Lara, thus putting an end to the constant public spectacle about their relationship. She had more money now than she knew what to do with, many sumptuous jewels, and her son, Enrique, was enrolled in one of the best boarding schools in the world. What did she have to fear as she steered toward these new horizons? There was a trial run in Argentina: she was there under the direction of Luis Cesar Amadori in an adaptation of Anatole France's *Le Calvaire d'une courtisane*. But there was nothing in it to move the film lover. In truth, Argentina was much more than a stepping-stone for her new career. Above all, it would provide an idyll for her and her partner, Carlos Thompson, and for, as she claimed, her secret meetings with a certain woman of stature, the president Evita Perón.

Yet she felt that glamorous, intimidating Europe was awaiting her. She went to Spain, where her records and films were popular. But Franco reigned at the time, and his rigorous regime did not know what to do with this sensual gift from a cousin on the other side of the Atlantic. Therefore, the projects she shot there were rather calamitous, though *La Corona Negra* (1951), by the hardworking Luis Saslavsky, was honored with the literary collaboration of Jean Cocteau. Nevertheless, for her, Spain would be the Spain of plazas, of Manolete and Dominguín—the new bullfighting idol who would dedicate a number of trophies to her, before, of course, choosing Lucia Bosé over her when it came to taking a wife. That was only a slight injury to María's self-esteem: why throw away her future on a single man, she said, when there were so many? The parties of the 1950s illuminated the European capitals, and everyone considered rather beautiful, amusing, or titled drank champagne until dawn and danced on the volcano of the Cold War. María Félix was one of them, not exactly an actress any longer, but a VIP, before the term existed—one of those creatures who seem to spend the essence of their time smiling in magazines while posing in the incredible luxury of Balenciaga dresses and rivers of Cartier diamonds.

mention has already been made of her romantic escapades, the sort that defied ordinary morality. Those would go hand in hand with an overwhelming sense of doom: one year after marrying her, Jorge Negrete suddenly died; Félix saw this—the death of someone she could rely on, on whose shoulder she could rest her sinner's head—as punishment for her dissolute existence. And, she thought, it was a little too similar to those melodramas they kept offering her and in whose scripts perverse authors would sometimes slip direct allusions to her private life. The shadow of Pablo, her venerated brother, then took hold of her thoughts and her nightmares. He, too, died tragically, either by suicide or murder, they didn't know, and María seriously began to think that in the mental entanglements of her persona there was a charged morbidity and a furious appetite for pleasure, not the banal emotional ups and downs that characterized most of human destiny, but the mark of a higher order. She was perhaps the praying mantis, the deadly spider that society portraitists began including in their most elegant images.

1
ike a sign, Carmine Galone at Cineccità had her take on the role of Messaline, a character that resembled her like a sister. Like Messaline, she was covered in heavy jewels; like Messaline, she led men to their destruction, and, like her, she cast a haughty, weary glance upon the world. Italian photographer to the stars Arturo Ghergo captured her in this disguise that perhaps was not one. She was splendid in an accoutrement that on someone else might have been carnivalesque. She took advantage of this modeling session in Ghergo's studio to have him execute a few private images, with her Afghan greyhound at her side, and at her feet, a young, curvy, furiously androgynous page. The name of this new companion? Frede: Fred with an *e*, the grand priestess of the nocturnal temple Carrol's, a nightclub on rue de Ponthieu, for women who had excluded men from their love lives. Was this another way for María to escape her infatuations with seducers of all stripes, eliminating them as potential creators of drama, large and small?

Leonor Fini was invited to celebrate the couple in a double portrait, while all of Paris delighted in scandalous gossip about them. María wanted to magnify what had become the object of sarcastic remarks and opprobrium. Wasn't she above and beyond accepted laws, goddess that she was? Nothing seemed to taint her, not even the mudslinging articles in the press that attempted to soil her image during her trial against Frede, when the two women separated, debating their respective iniquities.

Imperious, María demanded that Leonor Fini detach her portrait from that of the repudiated woman, and it was that half of the masterpiece that would be contemplated by Alex Berger, the powerful businessman who now entered her life.

S he could have chosen to stop appearing on-screen at this point, to stop struggling against advancing age (she was approaching forty) that would condemn her to be immobilized in increasingly sculptural roles that lacked any vitality. From afar, on her Mexican land, she contemplated her cinema which had changed, been ruined, and that allowed her and her characters to be lost in the antiseptic jungle of cosmopolitan productions. In the eyes of oblivious or uninformed film lovers, only Luis Buñuel embodied Mexican cinema in its totality. María filmed *La Fièvre monte à El Pao* (1959) under his direction, which was certainly not one of the great director's best films. The French actor Gérard Philipe, who was already ailing (this would be his last film) did what he could with the extravagant script in which, as usual, María played a great lover brutally destroyed by the forward movement of history. She would have been better off going back to those productions devoid of meaning, in which she could still, wear dressing gowns as luxurious as evening gowns, evening gowns cut lower than nightgowns, and frivolous hats decorated with feathers. Surrounding her, as in her life (the life of luxury that her fourth husband offered her), were all deep sofas, stylish furniture, Baroque statues, and glittering crystal candelabras. Then it was a question of coveting diamonds and crushing men beneath her feet. Life as usual...

b ut none of this was important to her any longer. Now it was much more exciting to enjoy, without shame, her position as a satisfied wife and everything it brought in replenished abundance: the most flattering friend-ships, and compliments from the powerful people of the world, which the former little girl from Sonora never tired of hearing. Horse races, art openings, fashion shows, candlelit dinners— these were the settings in which she moved, like so many illuso-ry stage sets. Her partners were Farouk of Egypt, Ali Khan, and baron Guy de Rothschild. Twenty years of euphoria during which the actress gradually faded away in favor of a myth that was not supported by any outstanding work, except for the impressive gallery of portraits with which María decorated her homes. Like Oscar Wilde's Dorian Gray, she was content to observe the eternal radiance of her frozen beauty, set in a riot of fantastic symbols. There were no masterpieces here either: as on-screen, the brilliance of the model compensated for any pictorial tem-perament. No doubt she saved a few sketches from her romantic adventure with Diego Rivera and Frida Kahlo, sketches worthy of a museum, but she very calmly stated that she had always valued their passion over their painting. She much preferred the work of her friends Leonor Fini, Leonora Carrington, and Stanislao Lepri, skilled surrealist painters whose decorative universes blended perfectly with her collections of furniture and tapestries, porcelain and silver. In the later years, there would also be the creations of her last companion, Antoine Tzapoff, who painted a mythological María Félix, sanctified and adorned—like those religious statues that the pious dress in various costumes—in all the sartorial artifice imaginable.

i n this theatrical fantasyland, there was a single truth: the son who grew up as devoted to his mother as she was to him, whom she naturally hoped would escape the condition of being merely the son of a star. Yes, that he would remain authentic, as well as a living witness of an entire life of determined work against the fate inflicted on the poor. Félix hoped that he would join the world of intellectuals that had always captivated her, though she had only garnered praise from it that was too out of proportion to be truly sincere, or that was a bestial echo of desires more burdensome than honorific. Of course, her Enrique would graduate from the Institut des Sciences politiques; he would become one of those minds that María hoped would dominate and manipulate the society of men, far from the lights under which she spent her time. Her displeasure was palpable when the young man, sweeping aside his diplomas, announced his intention to follow her into acting. But her disappointment passed quickly. She was not sorry to be able to offer Enrique advice at the dawn of an artistic trajectory worthy of that of his mother's, advice that was magisterial.

And indeed, for the Mexican public, another star with the last name of Félix was born and shined during the sixties and beyond: Enrique Álvarez Félix. María, won over and happy, saw the new star rise to the heavens and became his closest adviser. Quique, her first and last passion. He, too, had developed a love for her in childhood that did not cease to grow, so much so that it could barely be expressed. He collected her films and everything his mother's fame had incited in the press. He had all her photos. As soon as he could, he would turn them into the elements of an album dedicated to her, *Una Raya en el Agua*, and, for him, she would agree to date the documents that would reveal her real age. Because, at over 75 years of age (the book would be published in 1992), she had not abandoned any of the coquetry of her gender and still chose clothes, had her hair done, and put on makeup as she had in the time of her splendor. Despite this, and along with other artifices, the rectangle of her face was accentuated to the point of giving her the strange rigor of a ritual mask, the enchantment of a sorceress. The cupola of her forehead stood out before the still dark mass of hair that had receded. She remained magnificent, however, fascinating, full of a ferocious will to live and to shine, always and forever.

alex Berger, her spouse of almost twenty years, died in 1974. A widow once again, María did not confine herself in the shimmering cocoon of her apartments and in her admiration for Enrique's success. Secret queen of a republican Mexico, she chaired events, traveled constantly, and began to be the subject of those tributes that mark both the twilight of a career and its inscription in the collective memory. She once again saw images of her forty-seven films at the counters of art-movie houses and wondered which was her real self: the one she now dragged around with her with some effort, or the one moving on-screen, who continued to look men over with a sovereign insolence and who, suddenly, could collapse and dissolve in a torrent of despair. And while these two Marías were famously superimposed at times, how—she asked and we ask—could the immarcescible idol that she had become still have something within her that sustained an unspecified pain?

Fate would provide a cruel response to that question. Enrique passed away in 1996, struck by a heart attack. María left Paris, masked in enormous black glasses behind which the Mexican people watched for tears that they would never see. It seemed as though she had transformed into that rock of dead souls, the *Peñón de las Animas* from the title of her first film; like those royal figures who must not allow their strongest emotions to filter through, she showed her public only proud impassiveness, a supreme disdain for those dark forces linking her to mere mortals.

She no doubt saved the tears and sobs for the solitude in which she found refuge. In memory of Enrique, she had a final resting place built in Cuernavaca, a sort of tomb in which she gathered her most precious belongings as a fairy-tale offering to the dearly departed and no doubt as a shrine to the phantom she had become. She wandered around there, amid a stupefying riot of rare objects and in a dusting of gold and bright colors that formed a halo around her entire life. And how long, how very long, this life was turning out to be! Did she have the power to prolong it as she saw fit, to decide her death, as Octavio Paz wrote, as she had once decided her rebirth? The world had changed, Mexico had changed, but she remained the Amazon with the heart of stone, this exceedingly beautiful "centauress" whose path no human could claim to equal, and whose abandonment no one could know.

Sometimes, in the secrecy of her isolation or for the spectacle of a televised tribute to her, she would dress in one of those dazzling folkloric costumes in which the cinema of the golden years had immortalized her. She would pretend to hear and be moved by an old standard by Agustín Lara, one that was inspired by her, ground out by a scratched record. But, above all, she liked nothing more than to curl up on one of her voluptuous sofas, open her jewelry boxes, and extract the heavy, fluid serpent made of diamonds that jewelers at Cartier had designed especially for her. She also cherished her emerald-studded crocodiles, her eyes lighting up at the fire of the gems spread around her. And if an interviewer dared ask her for some confidence concerning her career or lifestyle, she responded cynically, in a voice that was still deep: "I'm not an example of anything!"

And then she faded away, as in a long dissolve, in 2002, finally uniting the two María Félixes in one, already erected as a national heroine by her compatriots, a symbol of absolute, Baudelairean beauty by her admirers the world over—those who tirelessly revived the twenty-four images per second distilled by the 4,230 minutes in which she radiated her inimitable light through the cold matter of film, forever the *Doña*, la *Doña*, a whip raised high above the veneration of poor men.

collier de
chien

bracelet des Indes

Tsapoff 1992

LE GROUPE DES QUATRE
présente

GÉRARD PHILIPE
MARIA FÉLIX
JEAN SERVAIS

DANS

LA FiÈVRE
monte
A
EL PAO

BERTRAND

UNE RÉALISATION DE **LUIS BUNUEL**
D'APRÈS LE ROMAN DE **HENRY CASTILLOU**
PUBLIÉ PAR LES ÉDITIONS ALBIN MICHEL
ADAPTATION DE **LUIS BUNUEL , LUIS ALCORIZA , CHARLES DORAT , LOUIS SAPIN**

DIRECTEUR DE LA PHOTOGRAPHIE **GABRIEL FIGUEROA**
PRODUCTEUR DÉLÉGUÉ **RAYMOND BORDERIE** (C.I.C.C)
MUSIQUE DE **PAUL MISRAKI**
UNE CO-PRODUCTION FRANCO-MEXICAINE **GROUPE DES QUATRE** (PARIS)

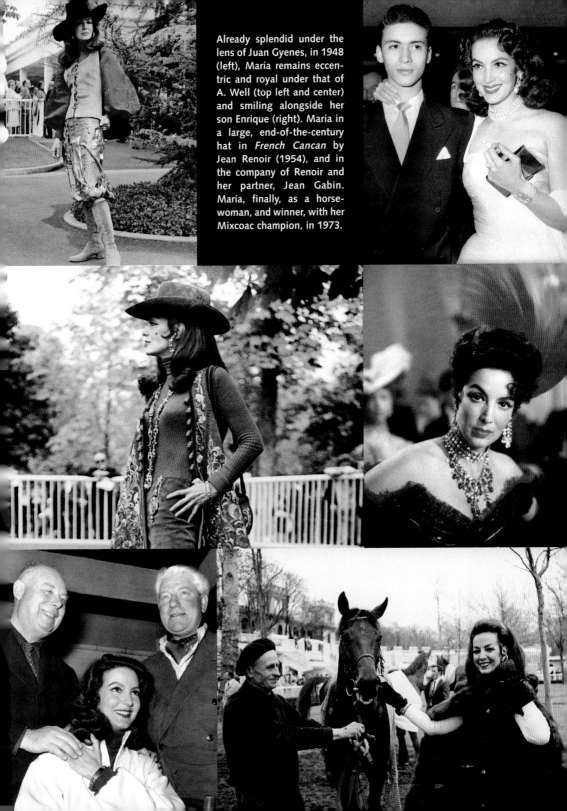

Already splendid under the lens of Juan Gyenes, in 1948 (left), María remains eccentric and royal under that of A. Well (top left and center) and smiling alongside her son Enrique (right). María in a large, end-of-the-century hat in *French Cancan* by Jean Renoir (1954), and in the company of Renoir and her partner, Jean Gabin. María, finally, as a horsewoman, and winner, with her Mixcoac champion, in 1973.

A voir !

Mix

Paris

Maille

Machoir

Biography

1914:   April 8: The birth of María de los Angeles Félix Güereña at ranch El Quiriego in Alamos (in the state of Sonora), daughter of Bernardo Félix (a descendant of Yaqui Indians) and Josefina Güereña (of Spanish descent, raised in a convent in Pico Heights, California).

1931:   María Félix marries Enrique Álvarez, a cosmetics salesman.

1934:   The birth of her son, Enrique Álvarez Félix.

1938:   Just after her divorce, María arrives in Mexico City, where she works as a receptionist for a plastic surgeon.

1940:   María meets Fernando Palacios who introduces her to the world of cinema.

1942:   She plays her first role in *Peñón de las Animas*, with the great Mexican actor of the time, Jorge Negrete.

1943:   María marries the Mexican composer Agustín Lara.

1946:   She receives the Ariel (the Mexican cinematic award) for best actress in the film *Enamorada*.

1947:   She divorces Agustín Lara.

1948:   She receives the Ariel for best actress in the film *Río Escondido*.

1950:   She receives the Ariel for best actress in the film *Doña Diabla*.

1952:   October 18: Marriage to actor Jorge Negrete.

1953:   December 5: Death of Jorge Negrete.

1956:   December 20: Marriage to the French businessman Alex Berger. Alex builds her a house in Polanco and gives her 87 horses that will win several prizes (including the French Jockey, the Grand Jockey of Dublin, the Prix Rond and the Steeplechase of Paris). They live there six months out of the year, residing in Paris the other six months (in an apartment situated near the Arc de Triomphe).

1974:   December 31: The death of Alex Berger.

1981:   Félix meets French painter Antoine Tzapoff.

1984:   The National Chamber of Fashion in Italy and the Federation of Haute Couture in France recognize her as one of the best-dressed women in the world.

1986:   She receives the "Diosa de Plata" award (given annually by Pecime, a jury of Mexican journalists who specialize in cinema to salute her entire cinematic career).

1992:   ANDA (the national association of Mexican actors) pays tribute to María Félix for her fifty-year career in film.

1996:   Her son Enrique passes away of a heart attack.
The thirteenth International Festival of Women in Film in Créteil pays tribute to María's career.
France names her Commander in the French Order of Arts and Letters.

1997:   María is the guest of honor at the first Film Festival of Madrid.

2002:   April 8: The death of María Félix in her home at Polanco, outside Mexico City, at the age of 88.

Filmography

1942
- *El Peñón de las ánimas* by Miguel Zacarías.
- *María Eugenia* by Felipe Gregorio Castillo.

1943
- *Doña Bárbara* by Fernando de Fuentes and Miguel M. Delgado.
- *La China poblana* by Fernando Palacios.
- *La Mujer sin alma* by Fernando de Fuentes.

1944
- *Amok* by Antonio Momplet.
- *La Monja alférez* by Emilio Gómez Muriel.

1945
- *El Monje blanco* by Julio Bracho.
- *Vértigo* by Antonio Momplet.

1946
- *Enamorada* by Emilio Fernández.
- *La Devoradora* by Fernando de Fuentes.
- *La Mujer de todos* by Julio Bracho.

1947
- *La Diosa arrodillada* by Roberto Gavaldón.
- *Que Dios me perdone* by Tito Davison.
- *Río Escondido* by Emilio Fernández.

1948
- *Maclovia* by Emilio Fernández.
- *Mare Nostrum* by Rafael Gil.

1949
- *Doña Diabla* by Tito Davison.
- *Una Mujer cualquiera* by Rafael Gil.

1950
- *La Noche del sábado* by Rafael Gil.

1951
- *Incantésimo trágico* by Mario Sequi.
- *La Corona negra* by Luis Saslavsky.
- *Mesalina* by Carmine Gallone.

1952
- *La Pasión desnuda* by Luis César Amadori.

1953
- *Camelia* by Roberto Gavaldón.
- *El Rapto* by Emilio Fernández.
- *Reportaje* by Emilio Fernández.

1954
- *La Bella Otero* by Richard Pottier.
- *French Cancan* by Jean Renoir.

1955
- *Canasta de cuentos mexicanos* by Julio Bracho.
- *La Escondida* by Roberto Gavaldón.
- *Les Héros sont fatigués* by Yves Ciampi.

1957
- *Faustina* by José Luis Sáenz de Heredia.
- *Tizoc* by Ismael Rodríguez.

1958
- *Café Colón* by Benito Alazraki.
- *Flor de mayo* by Roberto Gavaldón.
- *La Cucaracha* by Ismael Rodríguez.
- *La Estrella vacía* by Emilio Gómez Muriel.
- *Miércoles de ceniza* by Roberto Gavaldón.

1959
- *La Fièvre monte à El Pao* [*Fever Mounts at El Pao*] by Luis Buñuel.
- *Sonatas* by Juan Antonio Bardem.

1960
- *Juana Gallo* by Miguel Zacarías.

1962
- *La Bandida* by Roberto Rodríguez.
- *Si yo fuera millonario* by Julián Soler.

1963
- *Amor y sexo* by Luis Alcoriza.

1965
- *La Valentina* by Rogelio A. González.

1970
- *La Generala* by Juan Ibáñez.

María Félix

"Here are fruits, flowers, leaves and branches..." Like an image out of the poetry of Verlaine, María emerges from the garden created by Chávez Marión (left, *Saliendo del Jardín*. © Private collection of María Félix), wrapped in the benefits of nature. Isn't she herself one of these fruits, one of these flowers, one of these offerings of nature to the admiration and appetite of men? (right: © Private collection of María Félix).

María Félix could put aside a too perfect beauty to take on the mask of those women in the Americas who—alongside their male counterparts—took part in the revolutions. One example, on the left, is her expression in *Río Escondido* by Emilio Fernández (1948. © Gabriel Figueroa), the face of a heroine whose brothers could be Mexican peasants, right, photographed by Hugo Brehme in the 1920s (*Dos campesinos* © Hugo Brehme/Throckmorton Fine Arts).

The mythical image of the walking *soldadera*, holding on to the saddle of the horse ridden by her man, the soldier in *Enamorada* (Emilio Fernández, 1946) played by Pedro Armendariz. From now on, it will be María Félix in the historical role of a Mexican woman fighting for her freedom and that of her country. © Televisa, S.A. de C.V.

Cinema and painting correspond: María Félix in a Tehuana costume as seen by Antoine Tzapoff, left, in 1991 (© Private collection of María Félix), based on the memory of Félix as she was eternally captured in her role in *Enamorada*, right, at the feet of the cavalier Pedro Armendariz (© Collection Christophe L).

The *Doña* in all her haughty beauty and the austerity of her clothing and carriage: *Vértigo* by Antonio Momplet (1946). © Televisa, S.A. de C.V.

María Félix in *Quand gronde la colère* by Ismael Rodríguez, 1957. © Collection Raymond Boyer/ASTORIA Films.
María by Tzapoff. Her companion of the last years will accentuate the goddess that Félix became, as in this sketch for *María y Pedro* (1992). © Courtesy Antoine Tzapoff.

76

María Félix in *Canasta de cuentos mexicanos* by Julio Bracho, 1955: Julio Bracho's first film in color and cinemascope presents three tales drawn from the work of Bruno Traven, *La Révolte des pendus* (1936). María appears in the third of these tales (*La Tigresa*), alongside Pedro Armendáriz. © Akg Images.

María Félix at the height of her sex appeal, in this photographic study by Philippe Halsman (left) for *Esquire* magazine (© All Rights reserved). And in the role of Manuela (right), the exceedingly adventurous beauty, in *Les héros sont fatigués* by Yves Ciampi, 1955 (Raymond Boyer Collection. Photograph: Roger Corbel © Ministry of Culture). This was a story of alcohol and diamonds, the kind that were popular at the time, in which, before dying, María inevitably found her place, and no less inevitably, relinquished her chance with the hero, Yves Montand.

Les héros sont fatigués, the heroes are tired, often, but María is always there to encourage their evil ways, before dying as a result (Raymond Boyer Collection. Photograph: Roger Corbel © Ministry of Culture). She will die for Yves Montand, and she will die for Gérard Philipe, under the watchful gaze of Luis Buñuel, in *Fever Mounts at El Pao* of 1959 (© All Rights reserved).

The transformation of María Félix. In several films and after ten years of effort to experience a rebirth, the blossoming star now managed to exist by her presence alone and the mysterious chemistry of light on the architecture of a face. (left: María Félix in the 1940s. © Manuel; right: in the 1950s. © Photofest).

Painters who are also friends: Diego Rivera, abandoning political painting for one canvas, sees María this way in *Muy Malo* of 1949 (left: private collection of María Félix. © 2006 Banco de México Diego Rivera & Frida Kahlo Museums Trust. Av. Cinco de Mayo, No 2, Col. Centro, Del. Cuauhtémoc 06059, México, D.F.). Leonor Fini will be the awe-struck chronicler of her Parisian visit and creator in the 1950s of Reina del Fuego, one of the many portraits of María (right: *Queen of Fire*. © All Rights reserved).

Even in the Latino-detective story folklore of *Les héros sont fatigués* by Yves Ciampi (1955), **María Félix, breaking with convention, portrays a statue-like character** who displays the impassibility of a diva endangered in a foreign land. Raymond Boyer Collection. Photograph: Roger Corbel © Ministry of Culture.

Already splendid under the lens of Juan Gyenes, left, in 1948 (© Biblioteca Nacional, Madrid), María remains eccentric and royal under that of A. Well (top left and center, © A. Well) and smiling alongside her son Enrique (© Roger-Viollet). María in a large, end-of-the-century hat in *French Cancan* by Jean Renoir (1954. © Serge Beauvarlet), and in the company of Renoir and her partner, Jean Gabin (© Rue des Archives). María, finally, as a horsewoman, and winner, with her Mixcoac champion, in 1973 (© All Rights reserved).

In the city as well as on the stage, María cultivates a perfectly sophisticated, sublimely feminine Latin beauty (left, in *La Belle Otero* by Richard Pottier, 1954. Photograph: Roger Corbel © Ministry of Culture; right: © All Rights reserved).

In Jean Renoir's *French Cancan* (1954), María is given the task of representing the poisonous charm of the great courtesans of the Belle Epoque. She is the remote and arrogant star of a new Moulin Rouge, where diplomats and ministers fight over her favors, in a storm of her scorn and anger. A role that was tailor-made for her. © All Rights reserved.
María, as a woman-bird, as seen by Stanislao Lepri in *María Pájaro*, 1964. © Private collection of María Félix.

María's extraordinary villa in Cuernavaca, called Las Tortugas (The Tortoises), which she decorated as she pleased. © All Rights reserved.
And María, looking pensive, during the shooting of *Juana Gallo* by Miguel Zacarías in 1961. © Allan Grant/Time Life Pictures/Getty Images.

The patio and swimming pool of Las Tortugas in Cuernavaca, 2001. The photograph appeared in the magazine *Casas & Gente*. © Casas & Gente.

Jean Cocteau wrote *La Couronne noire* (The Black Crown) for María, which was directed by Luis Saslavski in 1951. Félix, pursued by death, is divided between transalpine sex symbols Rossano Brazzi and Vittorio Gassman. Featuring the dwarf Piéral, who is meant to convey the poet's fantasies, from Paris to Tangier. © All Rights reserved.

The gold of the Venetian living room at Las Tortugas (Cuernavaca, 2001), presided over by the *Allegory of America* by Antoine Tzapoff. The photograph was published in the magazine *Casas & Gente*. © Casas & Gente.
Self-portrait of the couple, María Félix and Antoine Tzapoff, for a painting entitled *Allegory of America*, 1986. © Private collection of María Félix.

78

Detail of a portrait of María Félix by Antoine Tzapoff (1985). She is wearing an ornamental headdress given to her by Jeanne Toussaint, creative director of Cartier. © Courtesy of Antoine Tzapoff.
Another glimpse of the swimming pool at Las Tortugas. © All Rights reserved.

María with her necklace of coral, diamonds, emeralds, and onyx, created by Cartier in 1940, and her bulky, clip-on earrings, created in 1966. (left: © All Rights reserved; right: © Cartier).

María, triumphant owner of a stable of race horses, at the Grand Prix of the Arc de Triomphe at the Longchamp hippodrome, October 4, 1959. © Rue des Archives.
María in *Fever Mounts at El Pao* by Luis Buñuel, 1959. © All Rights reserved.

María Félix in 1960. © Allan Grant/Time Life Pictures/Getty Images.
María Félix: the muse. In 2006, Cartier pays homage to her by creating the "La Doña de Cartier" watch. © Cartier.

Detail of a portrait of María Félix created after a picture of Lord Snowdon. The Mexican actress wears her *Crocodiles* necklace, diamonds, emeralds ordered in1975. Courtesy of Isabelle Rey, 2005 .© Cartier.
The Crocodiles necklace: 1,023 yellow diamonds and 1,060 emeralds, a special order made by the Cartier workshops in 1975. Photograph: Nick Welsh/Collection Cartier. © Cartier.

A surrealist portrait of María Félix by Stanislao Lepri: *La Última Jugada* [The last part], 1964. © Private collection of María Félix.
The last part Félix would play with fury great passion until her death in 2002, under a golden parasol and in the shimmering, rich fabrics of her native land. © All Rights reserved.

The publisher wishes to thank Mr. Javier Mondragón Alarcón and Mr. Luis Martínez de Anda in particular for supporting us with this project by giving us access to photographic documents from María Félix's private collection.
The publisher also wishes to thank Jaime Aguilar Alvarez (Televisa), Anouck Baussan (Getty Images), Jérôme Beauvarlet, the Biblioteca Nacional of Madrid, Anne-Catherine Biedermann (Ministry of Culture), Kraige Block (Throckmorton Fine Arts), Raymond Boyer, Serge Darmon (Collection Christophe L), Gabriel Figueroa, Fabienne Grevy (Akg Images), Donatella Lockhart and Leticia Gurrola Martinez (*Casas & Gente*), Barbara Mazza (Roger-Viollet), Christophe Mirambeau, Isabelle Rey, Alejandro Ruiz Cárdenas (Diego Rivera Estate), Ángeles Sánchez Gutiérrez and Graciela Sada (Cineteca Nacional of Mexico, Catherine Terk (Rue des Archives) and Antoine Tzapoff.